PENGUIN BOOKS

THE SUPPORT GROUP MANUAL

Harriet Sarnoff Schiff is the author of two classic works on grieving, *The Bereaved Parent* and *Living Through Mourning*, as well as *How Did I Become My Parent's Parent?* A former reporter for the *Detroit News*, she has lectured throughout the United States, Canada, and Australia, and has appeared on television shows such as "Donahue," "The Oprah Winfrey Show," and the "Today" show. More recently, as Corporate Admissions Coordinator for a group of thirteen nursing homes, she worked with admissions personnel and social workers, and ran activity programs and support groups for residents and family members. She lives in Birmingham, Michigan.

Harriet Sarnoff Schiff

THE SUPPORT GROUP MANUAL

A Session-by-Session Guide

PENGUIN BOOKS

PENGUIN BOOKS
Published by the Penguin Group
Penguin Books USA Inc., 375 Hudson Street,
New York, New York 10014, U.S.A.
Penguin Books Ltd, 27 Wrights Lane,
London W8 5TZ, England
Penguin Books Australia Ltd, Ringwood,
Victoria, Australia
Penguin Books Canada Ltd, 10 Alcorn Avenue,
Toronto, Ontario, Canada M4V 3B2
Penguin Books (N.Z.) Ltd, 182–190 Wairau Road,
Auckland 10, New Zealand

Penguin Books Ltd, Registered Offices:
Harmondsworth, Middlesex, England

First published in Penguin Books 1996

LIBRARY OF CONGRESS CATALOGING IN PUBLICATION DATA
Schiff, Harriet Sarnoff.
    The support group manual: a session-by-session guide/Harriet
Sarnoff Schiff.
      p.   cm.
    ISBN 0 14 02.3715 1 (pbk.)
    1. Group counseling.   I. Title.
BF637.C6S32   1996
158'.35—dc20   96–5602

Printed in the United States of America
Set in Bembo
Designed by Fritz Metsch

Foreword

The support group manual created by Harriet Sarnoff Schiff is an informed, candid, and practical guide, uniquely blended valuable experience with specific direction to assist anyone confronting issues related to loss and life transition.

The manual should be read by both the provider and receiver of care, as it presents an encouraging, refreshing view of the value of support groups in healing and growth.

It has been my experience in working with groups founded by Harriet Sarnoff Schiff that many have benefited and gained positive and long-term support.

Marilyn Kuperus Gilbert, Ph.D.

A Word of Welcome

A friend is a present you give yourself.

The support group is about friendship. It is about kinship. It is something in which to take pride.

You are unique. Not everyone is willing to give themselves the gift of good listeners who are understanding and not judgmental.

You are unique because you feel you are deserving of such interactions.

You are unique because you are willing to share some of yourself so others may grow and learn and be more comfortable.

You are unique because you understand that in belonging to the group you belong to an entity that you can define.

You are unique because you can identify by name the people who are willing to accept your pain, just as you are willing to accept theirs.

Most of all, you are unique because you have enough strength to take the plunge and join with others who feel what you are feeling.

Remember, being with a group of people experiencing a similar pain will not add to your own pain. Instead it will divide it among all those who attend.

Although you are feeling many emotions, such as deep sorrow or frustration or pain, you have made a conscious decision not to wallow alone in your hurt. Wallowing alone can be like trying to swim out of quicksand without someone to throw you a rope.

As a member of a support group, you will be amazed to find that total strangers may share more intimately with you than they have with their nearest and dearest family and friends. You will be equally surprised to find yourself doing the same.

Acknowledgments

With appreciation to CBS's "Sunday Morning" for televising a meeting of the Bereavement Support Group of Temple Israel in West Bloomfield, Michigan.

Thank you to Rabbi M. Robert Syme and Rabbi Harold Loss, Rabbi Dannel Schwartz for his insights and to Rabbi Michael Moscowitz for his current perspective. Also, to the many clergy of different faiths, medical people, and mental health people who have believed in what I was doing and who have found the support groups useful.

To those who have benefited from the support groups, my appreciation for your input and your sharing with me how you were helped.

And, of course, to Sander, who is my support.

Contents

Contents

Introduction
to Support Groups and
the Philosophy

People experience as many losses today as they have throughout history. What makes coping with these losses more difficult in the late twentieth century is that our society has become so transient. Families no longer live in neighborhoods or enclaves. Instead they are scattered across the country and sometimes around the world.

When this country experienced great influxes of immigration, there was still continuity to be found in many neighborhoods. People came and stayed with family or others who shared a common language or heritage. There were Polish neighborhoods, Italian neighborhoods, Irish neighborhoods, Jewish neighborhoods—the list could go on and on. There was a sense of belonging, despite loneliness and, frequently, poverty.

People shared common experiences and difficulties. Even those who came to this country without knowing a soul did not feel so alone during times of stress and pain, because they were part of a community.

Our society today has become fragmented. That is why the support group has grown in importance and why there is such a need for it. A group provides a way for people to experience the connecting and sharing that are a vital part of the human condition.

The support group is for all those who feel hurt and powerless and ineffectual and alone. The group is an affirmation that no one walks alone who chooses to share his or her life with others.

Everyone experiences pain in a different way, yet there are enough commonalities to make a group cohesive.

If a group works well, it will become a gathering of friends who speak freely in front of one another. Many people have no other outlets for speaking freely.

In many cases, family and friends have heard the same pain repeated far too often for them to continue being supportive. People lose patience and begin to drift out of the lives of those who stay focused on one topic continually. This does not mean that these support people are not caring. It simply means they have heard as much as they are capable of taking in. But you may now feel more alone than ever.

Old sayings stay with us because they are held together with the glue of years of testing. That is certainly the case when we remind ourselves that there is strength in numbers.

In coming to a support group, you have decided you will no longer bear the responsibility for tough decisions alone. Nor is it necessary to add the panic of feeling alone to an already painful situation.

The group will move slowly, at a pace that is comfortable for the participants. It is not urgent that you plunge immediately into deep problem areas.

In fact, learning to pace yourself can ease some of the pain.

Because in this culture we are so accustomed to doing things quickly, we tend to hurry through nearly all aspects of our lives, including dealing with loss. When we are lonely for someone, we can simply pick up the telephone and call the person we miss. Coping with loss requires us to slow down. When you recognize there are no instant solutions, that your healing will indeed be gradual, you will be better able to see the progress you make.

One thing is certain: with each meeting, you will come closer to resolving your difficulty, regardless of which area of stress you are addressing.

Support group meetings are held every week in the same place on the same day or evening. The reason for this structure is to bring continuity back into lives that are fractured.

As you enter a support group, try to do three important things:

Look around and see the faces of the others in your group. They are a mirror of your own. See their posture. Note how you yourself sit or lean. If you observe someone who has a carriage you admire, try to sit that way or lean that way. You may find strength in making even those small changes in yourself.

Listen to what is said by your fellow group members. It is not productive for you to be planning what you will say when it is your turn to speak. That will come quite naturally. Instead pay close attention to what others say. You will be surprised by how frequently their words are the balm your heart needs.

Learn the value of different perspectives. Sometimes an idea that completely eludes you is quite obvious to another group member. Try not to negate an idea just because it sounds strange or too difficult to grasp upon first hearing. You are in pain now, and it is possible that a different approach to an idea can make it click within you.

Although there is a proven agenda for a group to follow, which this book will lay out, if you have something to discuss that pertains to a previous meeting, it should be addressed before the new session topic is introduced.

You are embarking on a new experience. If you have always been a private person, this will be an adventure of some magnitude. It is my hope that by participating in a group you will experience personal growth and acquire new ways of handling problems.

You will come with a heavy heart, but you will leave with a loving heart that will open you to new experiences and ideas, and to friendships with those you have come to know.

There will be some meetings that will leave you drained because they touch on topics that are raw. If that is the case, do something physical when you get home.

Do not sit down in front of your television set or go to bed. Scrub a floor or clean an oven. If you cannot do heavy work, organize drawers and shelves.

Do something. You will feel that you are taking charge. When you can see positive outcomes in a short period of time as a result of your efforts, you will feel stronger and more in charge of events in your life.

Most important, remember that a support group is never a substitute for private counseling. If you see that the group is discussing things at one level, while you are experiencing extraordinary pain and stress that is well beyond what you are hearing, please consider counseling. You need not leave the group. It is generally possible to do both.

If your group facilitator suggests you see someone for private therapy, understand that you are not being brushed aside but that the facilitator sees you might have some special needs that only individual therapy can meet. If finances are a problem, nearly every community has a social service organization with a sliding fee scale.

On the other hand, there are many people who suffer a loss but do not need one-on-one therapy. They need a good ear—a sounding board. The support group offers them this opportunity. Also, it is sometimes easier to share strong emotions, especially when there has been great disappointment, with people outside of one's own circle.

A support group is more than a coffee klatch and less than a therapy session. It is an excellent in-between into which the majority of people fit most comfortably.

Life is not fair. It never has been. But it has meaning if you allow meaning to be there. Take pride in who you are and in your willingness to grow and heal.

You have earned it.

My best wishes.

Is a Support Group for You?

A support group can comprise people dealing with the same issue or different issues. The common experience of loss or life transition among members is most often felt in one of the following situations.

Aging

Aging is a great equalizer. It does not matter whether one is rich or poor, accomplished or not accomplished. When you are in the throes of deciding "what to do about" your parent or spouse or sister or brother, it is inevitable that you will feel frustrated and powerless.

Aging is also an issue if you are doing the aging! In your heart you may feel thirty or forty, but your body and your memory are not going along with the program. From time to time they betray you. You blinked and you were twenty. You blinked again and you are sixty, seventy, or eighty. In a support group, others who have experienced just this sort of jolt will be there with you to explore feelings and work alongside you on practical methods of staying not young but comfortable with being your age.

Divorce

Whether you had a long-time marriage or relationship or one that lasted only a few years, you will probably feel a deep sense of loss when that relationship dissolves. You gave yourself to someone with every hope or even certainty that your decision would mean a lifelong bond.

When you discover that is no longer the case, that the marriage or relationship is over, regardless of the cause, it can be shattering, whether you are twenty or sixty. Others who have been down that road can help validate what you are feeling.

In a support group, you will almost invariably meet others who have parted from spouses or partners for any number of reasons: infidelity, physical abuse, substance abuse, incompatibility, broken promises. There is, indeed, a great bond between people who have lived with broken dreams until they could live with them no longer.

Career Loss

You probably grew up with the belief that you would receive a day's wages for a day's work. You were programmed to exhibit loyalty to your employer as part of the job agreement. On the other hand, your employer had a role to fulfill in providing the opportunity to earn a livelihood, helping workers meet the needs of their families, and in many cases creating a sense of well-being and self-esteem. Most of all, you believed that your corporate position or chosen field of work offered a reasonable amount of stability. You never expected to have to pound the pavement looking for work because of such things as downsizing.

You may have even viewed your employer—even a large, impersonal corporation—in an almost parental role. Now, with companies closing, moving to other cities, or merging with larger corporations, people are left out in the cold. For many, losing a job can be as traumatic as being let down by Mom or Dad.

Bereavement

We all are aware that life holds two certainties—death and taxes. (In some cases, we cannot be sure even taxes apply. While here and there you might find a tax dodger, you will never find someone who will not die!)

Like aging, death is a great equalizer. Despite medicines and fountain-of-youth spas all over the world, death is a normal part of the life process, and all of us will meet it someday.

Outwardly certain deaths seem more gut-wrenching than others. When a child dies, when a loved one has been murdered, or when a spouse of half a century dies, the survivor's sense of bereavement is always intense. Another dreadful sense of loss is experienced when a brother or sister dies. You may feel the emptiness of the place that missing person used to occupy.

You may have found that it is equally painful when a much-loved friend dies. There are times—since we cannot pick our relatives, but we certainly do select our friends—when such a loss feels nearly unbearable. What adds to the tragedy is that generally only family is acknowledged after a death. People rarely approach a grieving friend and extend condolences. The friend generally grieves alone and rarely receives needed support.

Illness

There are many other types of losses you may be dealing with, including serious and terminal illness.

An illness may involve you, or it may involve loved ones. People who have been given a serious or fatal diagnosis know how frightening this can be. Afraid and anxious, your response may have been, "Shall I keep it a secret?" or "I've got to call everyone and let them know."

Equally difficult—indeed some would say more difficult—is discovering that a loved one is seriously ill or is going to die within a predicted period of time. What do you say? How do you provide comfort when you yourself are in pain?

This is not the time to be alone. This is not the time to feel alone.

Alternative Lifestyles

There is also the loss caused by lack of acceptance. This is a situation that many in the gay community continue to experience. It is also frequently experienced by their family members. Each seems to lose the other and find it impossible to be supportive. Many gay people carry great resentment because they have felt the need to spend years hiding and denying, especially if they were hiding from parents and other immediate family members.

Often family members, as well as friends of the family, may feel uncomfortable with the gay lifestyle. They fear being "tainted" somehow by association, or wonder whether they are somehow "to blame." A difficult situation becomes worse because of hiding and fear and worry about what others will say and think.

Gays come to the support group issue differently than other groups because other groups are acknowledged and given their dignity. Society acknowledges the sufferings of a widow, a divorced person, an aging person, and thus grants them respect. Gays often have to find that respect internally in order to withstand those "slings and arrows" of bigotry that they face even today.

The greatest gift a family concerned with an alternative lifestyle can give themselves is to not stay separated from others, or from their gay family member— to strive to join with others working to accept gay friends and family.

People in this situation might benefit by creating a separate group for themselves first and, after completing that group, joining a general support group that focuses on loss.

Meeting One

DENIAL

Life is not a problem to be solved but a reality to be experienced.

—KIERKEGAARD

One of the hardest tasks we face in coping with denial is understanding it—seeing how it shapes and misshapes our lives.

The first session is the time to meet one another and begin the process of support. Each member will be asked

- What is your name?
- What type of life change are you experiencing?
- Is there someone that you need to come to terms about?
- What is his/her first name?
- What is your issue with that person or situation?

This sharing is your first step in telling people what is causing you pain. Not only does it help you get acquainted immediately, but the information also helps everyone in the group.

The fact that you have come to this meeting says you are ready to face reality, or at least put a toe in the water of truth.

Denial is our conditioned response to a situation that threatens to cause us great and immediate pain. One of the first things we say is, "No, I don't believe it." Denial that is allowed to persist unexamined can hamper the process of grief and mourning and ultimate healing.

If we cling to what is not true, we prevent ourselves from taking advantage of healing. We deny ourselves the opportunity to bring about change.

Picture someone clinging to the side of a sinking ship, afraid to let go. Awaiting that person is a lifeboat that is in fine working order and capable of escorting people to safety. But if a person cannot let go of the side of the ship and take that leap of faith into the lifeboat, he or she is in danger of sinking along with the vessel.

That person risks drowning.

Your facilitator will ask you if you recall experiencing denial, or its less conscious version, forgetting. Indeed many people within the group may still be getting flashes of this sensation. Are there times, perhaps the first thing in the morning, when you forget your pain? Then does it come over you in a sharp, searing manner? If so, share that with the group. Not only will you be helping yourself by verbalizing your own hurt, you will be helping someone else who fears his or her "forgetting" is not normal.

One of the primary comforts of the support group is that we discover just how "normal" we are, how many feelings we share in common, how often we are afraid and then afraid of our fear.

The group is helpful because it can be used as a measure of just where you are in the healing process.

There is also great value to all concerned if you have reached a point where you can look directly at your pain and not deny its existence.

If you can remember how you achieved this, share it with the group. Not only will you give yourself the benefit of reinforcing your own strength, you will also help others who are ready to hear what you have to say.

Many hurting people feel they are making some progress when they have gotten past denial. The sense that you are paddling, even without oars, can be exhilarating after feeling you were drowning in a vast, choppy ocean.

After reaching a certain age, when you realize you are forgetting names and events more frequently, you may panic and not wish to see the truth. People, as they get older, have begun to refer to this type of forgetting as "sometimers." Sometimes they remember and sometimes they do not.

Denial may be the sense of unreality you feel as you look at the stacked-up cartons that contain your former mate's belongings. Once you promised to be a couple, and now you are alone.

In any of these circumstances, you probably recall thinking or screaming aloud, "This is not happening!" Ironically, all that pain and horror you have experienced is often the beginning of the healing process.

Denial has been called nature's natural anesthetic. It is your effort not to internalize information. Only when you can come out from under this form of ether can you really begin the process of coming to terms with the issue that is troubling you.

Very often, the first smattering of dealing with denial will begin at or after the funeral or when the doctor's words have had a chance to sink in. Sometimes the first visit after placing someone in a nursing home can have a similar effect.

As you experience the pain, you come to grips with reality. The pain is like a dash of cold water. You are out of the anesthetic. That reality forces you, despite a hidden or overt unwillingness, to face the sad truth that your great difficulty is real.

In order to help you understand what you feel, your group facilitator will invite each of you to discuss a little of what you know about loss. You will be asked how old you were when you first had such an experience.

That loss can be of any intensity. All that is significant is that you experienced a certain pain of separation, whether from a pet, a friend, or a lost pair of shoes. The sensation is the issue.

It is helpful to discuss whether we shelter our young people from this process. After all, loss is something that happens to all of us at some time in our lives.

If the discussion is non-threatening and you begin from your early years, you can gradually work your way forward to the present.

Talking about who was helpful to you when you experienced a loss and *how* they were helpful can be valuable to the entire group.

Sometimes as a response to the urgency of denial, people become angry at those they perceive as authorities: teachers, doctors, clergy, superiors at the workplace, funeral directors, nursing home personnel, lawyers, or judges.

These are the people upon whom anger is frequently vented. If you have been in a situation that was handled by someone in authority in a manner you consider glaringly incorrect, talk it over with the group. Get some feedback.

You may decide to write a letter to the person in authority explaining your feelings. Do not simply send it to the institution. Find the specific person and address the letter to him or her.

By and large, people in positions of authority try as hard as they are able to make things comfortable. Of course, they do not always succeed, and if they do not, they should be told. You may well help the next person they deal with.

On the other hand, if you have had good, positive experiences, share them with the group and with the people who helped you. This can be very heartening to those who have the difficult task of dealing with people experiencing loss. What worked for you may help someone else.

Another issue that may be raised in the group is how to respond to the "things people say." In less emotional moments, you will surely recognize the difficulty people experience in responding to those who are suffering from pain and loss. But during moments of high intensity, few people display superhuman magnanimity. You probably recall a few trite sayings that were offered over and over again and that simply did not console.

Sometimes, in fact, they were downright outrageous.

As you will hear from others in the group, if you are newly suffering a loss you will need patience. Be prepared!

If you are widowed and someone offers you "comfort" by telling you that at least you had him for forty years, it takes great restraint not to lash out at that person. The people in the group will understand that when you love someone there is never enough time to be together.

On the other hand, the opposite situation frequently exists for people dealing with gay issues. They are frequently met with silence. As a rule, people have not yet figured out the appropriate things to say about this situation to someone who is coming to terms with an alternative lifestyle. As more and more people come out, foolish things will be said with great regularity. If you have been told something nonsensical, share it with the group. You will all benefit from hearing the words uttered in a safe and supportive setting.

Regardless of your issue, if you have had thoughtless things blurted out at you by people who are trying to say and do the right thing, share them with the group.

You may also wish to discuss responses. There are many angry, bereaved parents who have been told, "At least you have other children." It is nothing short of a miracle that these parents can calmly walk away from such insensitivity while feeling an inner rage.

These are some things to remember that might prove helpful:

- Restraint is admirable . . . and desirable.
- How did you handle foolish utterances?
- Did you smile and walk away?
- Did you rebuke someone?
- At another time, if the pain was not so intense, would you have laughed?

Perhaps your method will help someone else in the group who has not thought through as clearly as you have how to handle such situations.

If time permits, your facilitator will ask each of you whether you have handled the practical affairs that need to be addressed following a loss.

After a reasonable length of time, it is necessary to face the reality of your situation. If there has been a death, do not allow your home to become a mausoleum. If you face a serious illness, at least begin the business of healing or putting your affairs in order.

If you are newly divorced, perhaps it is time to go into a restaurant alone, even if you only sit at the counter. There is always a time to make a beginning.

If you are gay, begin to meet others who are part of your community, but do not limit yourself to only other gays.

If you have just discovered a loved one is gay and you are having difficulty with the situation, ask some other people who are gay to share with you how the response of loved ones—whether negative or positive —affected them. There may be such a person in your group. Hearing from someone to whom you have no emotional attachment can help you find clarity.

Everyone who has experienced an important death or other loss seems to hold on to some material thing or painful memory. Be assured that this is not unusual. A man whose leg has been amputated might well keep a trophy he won running a race years ago.

If you have experienced a loss or an alienation, your facilitator will ask you what you kept and why. What was its meaning to you? You may not even know, but possibly someone else in the group will have a theory about your decision that is worth exploring.

As your session comes to an end, the facilitator may share a prayer or special thought with you.

If you have comments on what has been read, share them with the group. Added insights are always valuable and welcome. If you come across any sayings or thoughts that may be of interest to the group, bring them next time.

At this meeting you have discussed denial. By exploring reactions to treatment by authority and to things people say, you have also gained insight into your fellow group members and how they think.

Your facilitator will ask you to bring photographs to the next session. Please do so if you are comfortable with it.

Remember, life can only be *understood* by looking backward. But life must be *lived* by looking forward.

Before the next meeting, think about what was discussed at this session. If you like, make notes on the page at the end of this section.

Also, if something comes to mind that you want to say at the next meeting, write it down.

When you next meet, the topic will be anger.

Things I Learned at This Meeting:

_____

_____

_____

_____

_____

_____

_____

The Point I Wish to Make at the Next Meeting:

_____

_____

_____

_____

_____

_____

_____

Meeting Two

Anger

He who will not reason is a bigot. He who cannot is a fool; and he who dares not is a slave. We must not become slaves to anger.

—ANONYMOUS

Because you addressed such a wide range of introductory topics at the first meeting, you may feel fairly well acquainted with the other members of the group.

Nevertheless, as at the previous session, you will be asked

- What is your name?
- What type of life change are you experiencing?
- Is there someone that you need to come to terms about?
- What is his/her first name?
- What is your issue with that person or situation?

There may be newcomers at this session, but after the following session that will not be the case. Take their newness into account and try to be as welcoming as possible.

Before turning to the topic of this session, your facilitator will invite you to contribute to an overview of what was discussed in the first meeting. This summary time will be helpful not only to those new to the group, but also to those who need to reiterate certain feelings about denial.

Explaining to the newcomers what you have experienced, as well as something of what the group has taught you, may help you discover a sense of ease within yourself.

If you do not wish to contribute to this portion of the meeting, you may still benefit simply by hearing certain issues restated and feelings reiterated.

Do, however, remember the time factor. The facilitator has a format to follow and this session's discussion is of equal urgency, for now you will be talking about anger.

Anger you experience while in grief or mourning or as it relates to any loss can sometimes have peculiar overtones. It does not hit us in ways we might expect. Anger does not mean simply rage when a doctor has made a mistake, for such anger you might anticipate and easily understand.

Although certainly the doctor, clergyman, lawyer, employer, or caregiver may indeed have disappointed you, shunned you, or not done what you wanted, these people may in other cases be only the obvious targets for the deeper hurts you are feeling.

Many people select a person or institution upon whom to vent anger when they are reeling with pain. Although they do not always do this consciously, they may find it allows them to focus and define their feelings.

- "The doctor should have done more."
- "The clergyman did not visit enough or do a proper eulogy."
- "The nursing home staff did not pay proper attention to my mother or other loved one."
- "The funeral director is nothing but a money-grubbing monster."
- "The lawyer didn't fight hard enough for me."
- "My supervisor knows I'm gay and makes me work all the bad hours."
- "I always felt I had complete job security, and now they've let me go to save those almighty dollars."

Such thoughts may have flitted through your head from time to time since your special person's situation changed or since your own life has undergone transition.

You may look around and feel powerless.

The facilitator will ask how you feel about the people you care about as well as the people in the various institutions you may have dealt with. He or she will inquire how you feel about the way they performed their functions. This is the time to share both negative and positive feelings.

Do you feel comfortable with how people have dealt

with you? Have you been listened to compassionately? Do you feel people have stopped displaying a strong interest in your feelings? Do you feel anger that you cannot focus? This is the place to share such feelings and hurts and disappointments.

Your facilitator will ask the group if others have felt similar emotions and what they did to help themselves.

If, for instance, a clergyman did something to offend you and you wish to share it, you may very much want to talk about it with the group.

The facilitator will ask the group how your situation could have been more appropriately handled. With their various experiences, the group participants may have excellent suggestions to offer. If there is a consensus, consider their words and perhaps incorporate their ideas into your thinking or into your letter, if you write one.

If you do choose to communicate to the person your disappointment with the way he or she has handled your situation, you help that person and others with whom he or she may come in contact if you are able to share alternative methods of handling a similar event.

Remember, however, that support group meetings are not and never were intended to be gripe sessions. They are designed to help people go forward.

Eventually you may come to see the value of knowing that someone else benefited from your anger and pain.

There is, in many of us, more anger than the obvious type we readily can touch or express. Often such anger is so devastating that you feel it must remain secret. You may fear it reflects badly upon you not only in the community at large, but in the deepest part of your own being.

That anger is the anger you may feel toward the person who is the focal point of your pain.

You are angry at your husband because he died.

You are angry at your child because he or she is gay and therefore may be considered a marginal member of society. You will never have grandchildren from this child, who held such promise as a youngster.

You may be angry because you are gay. Although it may be difficult to admit, you might prefer to be in the mainstream. You may be angry because you are not accepted the way your siblings are.

Now you have seen some of these thoughts on paper. They may make you squirm, but is there not a place deep down within you where the anger lies like an eternal flame that burns away at your consciousness and, indeed, your soul?

It is easier to get caught up in being angry at others—people to whom you can express your anger —than it is to be angry at the person about whom you feel loss.

Are you bypassing your true feelings, the feelings that are so secret that they must not be thought or felt?

You have probably been taught to speak only well of those who are aged or ill or dead. You have been taught to think well of authority figures. You must speak only kindly to your children about your former spouse. You must tolerate the snickers surrounding your gay child and the idea that somehow *you* did something "wrong." You must always conduct yourself on a higher plane if you are gay; after all, you do want to fit in *somewhere*.

No, the negative ideas about the situation must be held within, regardless of the toll on you!

But in the real world, the world where sainted mothers, fathers, spouses, children, and friends become incapacitated, it does not always work that way. Often there is an anger you experience toward the very person about whom you are so concerned . . . and, *yes*, that person may be you!

You may feel abandoned. You may feel that you or your loved one should have tried harder. Whether that "trying harder" was about caring for someone who died, or retaining mental and physical faculties, or remaining alive, or staying in a marriage that did not come together, or knowing a child can no longer hide in the straight world, many people experience a strong sense of loss, and that loss turns to anger.

Many people see it as a betrayal. "How could he have let this happen if he really loved me?"

Simply knowing these emotions exist in other people

may offer you some relief. You are not some cold, unfeeling monster. Instead you are trying to understand an honest emotion that has perplexed you since the onset of the problem.

You have probably asked yourself any number of times how in the world you could be angry because he is aging or ill or because he died. Not angry *that* he died but *because he died*.

The group setting provides a safe place to share this feeling with others who will not judge your emotions.

When your facilitator raises the issue of anger, if it indeed is something you feel, make it a point to add your own perspective. You may offer one sentence that will jog a feeling in a fellow group member. That one sentence can serve as a stabilizer for that person a month, two months, or even a year down the line. An implicit sense of trust builds because everyone benefits when everyone shares.

Although you may also be feeling anger toward God, please reserve your comments, if possible, for the next session, which will deal specifically with religion and feelings about God.

Instead use this session to deal with your feelings about the helping people with whom you have dealt and with the pain you experienced because someone you loved or still love is lost or because the circumstances of your life have radically changed.

Your anger can consume you. You must not let that happen. You have already lost enough.

You need not lose yourself.

The facilitator may now encourage you to share with other members of the group photographs you may have brought. If this is your first session, please bring your pictures of your special person to the next meeting.

Here is yet another of those sayings that have stood the test of time, one that is most apt in any discussion about anger: "The happiest people don't always have the best of everything. They just make the best of everything."

Things I Learned at This Meeting:

_____

_____

_____

_____

_____

_____

The Point I Wish to Make at the Next Meeting:

_____

_____

_____

_____

_____

_____

_____

Meeting Three

RELIGION

Religion is not asking. It is a longing of the soul.
—GANDHI

Because you are grieving, because you are in pain, you will probably not be surprised to know that such emotions are frequently interwoven with thoughts about your faith and about God.

It is not the group's function to encourage or promote a belief system. Instead the group can bring into the light the nagging discomfort you may be experiencing about this topic. When you have been raised with certain beliefs and now, at your greatest hour of challenge, you are questioning them, it can be helpful to know you are not alone.

Once again, your facilitator will ask each of you

- What is your name?
- What type of life change are you experiencing?
- Is there someone that you need to come to terms about?
- What is his/her first name?
- What is your issue with that person or situation?

Not only does this sharing continue to affirm your kinship with others in the group and ease communication, but it also allows you once again to tell people what is causing you pain.

Like most people, in the course of your life you have probably had a changing relationship with faith. You may have drawn closer to your faith, pulled away from it, or found a different faith or path that suits your needs.

This is not unusual, and that is most important to remember.

Equally important is knowing that people occasionally question their faith.

Following the death of a significant person or after enduring a life-altering event, some people will suddenly pull closer to God. Not only will they cling to their beliefs with fervor, they may also become more involved in rituals than ever before.

Other people, even some long-time observant religious people, will at such a turning point reject entirely the concept of God. They will shy away from any religious involvement, feel extreme bitterness toward God, and refuse to accept any comforting words that include a religious message or theme.

Still others examine their own faith and find it wanting. They search for and explore new avenues in order to find a more comfortable place that will ease the pain they are experiencing.

You may shift constantly. You may, in fact, love

The Support Group Manual

God one week and hate God the next—or decide there is no such thing as God!

After all, change is the result of discovering your feelings, and this can only be done by examining them. During the course of this session, you will be invited to share your views about God and perhaps about what your religion offers by way of comfort. It is your facilitator's job to make certain you are not put on the defensive, regardless of how you feel. Therefore speak freely and openly. Whatever your feelings, you have a right to them!

As you share your emotions and attitudes, try to be as coherent as possible. Try to explain clearly what you are experiencing to the group. Others will identify with what you are saying.

Also, be a good listener. Someone in the group may have something to share that will offer you a new insight. If your feelings are angry and hostile about religion, someone else who feels differently may explain why they are *not* angry. Listening with an open mind and heart will help you internalize new information that can be of value.

It is possible to restructure your beliefs. If you feel abandoned by God, someone may say something that will change that attitude.

Some people have never accepted the concept of a God. They may believe they live their lives according to appropriate moral and ethical principles, and look within for answers to life's stresses and tragedies.

As the discussion proceeds, you may feel that those who believe and cling to God at a hurting time are fortunate. At least for them not all is lost. Even if you do not feel such belief to be appropriate for you, it may clarify your feelings and be of help further down the road.

This discussion is one of the most challenging that support group members will encounter, and ideally it emphasizes the diversity of beliefs and opinions in your group. Things can become difficult, however, when people speak with the certainty that their way is the right and only path for everyone.

Statements such as "God had a greater plan" can send up a red flag. People who are in torment might well turn and respond that God is cruel and evil.

Someone else may say that we only have those we love because God lent them to us. This statement also can elicit venomous rage if presented awkwardly.

You will be asked how you feel about such ideas. Share your feelings and your reasons, but avoid personal attacks. See if you can keep the discussion on an intellectual level rather than one that is overwhelmed by emotions.

Discussions about religion usually include the concept of destiny. There are many people who believe

"What will be will be." You may be one of them. If that is how you perceive the events that have so pained you, share your views. Perhaps your attitude of acceptance can help someone think differently about their pain.

Always remember that any discussion about God must include an open mind or, at the very least, open ears.

Do not forget about the sensibilities of others in the group, and voice your views with kindness.

You may hear people—indeed even yourself—express anger toward God. For those who need to ventilate, there is no better forum than a support group.

On the other hand, if some wisdom has come to you since your painful experience, you should share that as well.

Talk about how your faith has helped you change, if that is the case. See if you can explain what makes you a different person today. What part did God play in this?

Since religion is a very sensitive topic, bear in mind that everyone in the group may wish to speak their minds, and time must be allowed for everyone. Try not to take offense if your facilitator indicates that he or she wishes to allow others in the session to share their experiences and thoughts.

If your belief in God is strong, you may find it difficult to listen to someone vilify God. You may sit there feeling defensive or angry or uncomfortable because you are hearing what you consider blasphemy.

A priest who deals well with grieving families once said, "It's okay to express your rage about the Lord. God has strong shoulders. God can take it. I feel no need to defend the Deity." Those with a strong belief in God might well embrace those words and learn from them.

If you do not believe in the existence of a supreme being or force, it can be equally difficult to listen to someone who keeps repeating, "This is the will of God." You can feel the anger growing within you at those words.

People who do not believe in God must also be given equal time to express their views. Perhaps you have prayed ceaselessly for the well-being of your special person. Then that person dies or changes in ways that are painful to observe. Not only do you feel the pain of the loss; you also have to find answers to the question "Why did this happen to me?"

You or others in the group may feel "rejected by God" because God did not listen to your prayer. That is not necessarily the case. God may well have listened. But God said no.

Often such people feel bitter at what they perceive as God's rejection. Such people are hurting. Please be kind. No one should be in a group to convert anyone else to their belief system.

At the end of this session, your facilitator will attempt to create some perspectives for all of you. He or she will try to summarize what has been said. Facilitators cannot answer your "Why?" or dissolve your pain. They can tell you what they have heard in your group and perhaps in other groups on this very sensitive topic. You might find the feedback helpful.

Of course, you will leave the meeting with much still on your mind about religion, but you should know that no matter how you are feeling at any given time, there is always someone out there who feels as you do.

Regardless of your personal beliefs about God, whether you need to hold on for support, opt to reject religion, doubt the existence of God, or believe human beings have only finite, objective existence, there is a coping skill that can be shared and learned.

If your group is affiliated with a religious organization, or even if it is not, you may wish to invite a minister, priest, or rabbi to come and share some biblical concepts and join the discussion for a session.

Generally clergy people are very willing to cooperate.

If you do invite a clergy person, make sure he or she understands that this is not a time for sermons, because that is not the function of the group. It is a time for people to seek answers and, it is hoped, to discover some ideas that are helpful.

Perhaps the clergy person has seen a family handle a

particular circumstance in a manner that proved effective. Sharing this with the group can be useful.

If you have brought photos of your special person, please share them with the group. Being able to envision each other's loved ones makes the discussions more personal.

Cardinal Newman said, "Fear not that life shall come to an end, but rather fear that it shall not have had a beginning." Since you are in pain, you probably view your events as an ending. As time goes on you may be blessed with the understanding that everything can offer a beginning.

Things I Learned at This Meeting:

_____

_____

_____

_____

_____

The Point I Wish to Make at the Next Meeting:

_____

_____

_____

_____

_____

_____

_____

Meeting Four

GUILT

For of all sad words of tongue or pen,
The saddest are these: "It might have been."
                              —JOHN GREENLEAF WHITTIER

Guilt is a very painful topic for people who grieve. We might paraphrase Whittier's lines by saying the saddest words are "If only I had." Whether real or imagined, guilt is a feeling that is almost universal to those who are hurting. Your openness about feeling guilty can help create a strong bond with other group members.

First, just to be certain everyone is settled in, each member will be asked

- What is your name?
- What type of life change are you experiencing?
- Is there someone that you need to come to terms about?
- What is his/her first name?
- What is your issue with that person or situation?

You may be experiencing intensely such thoughts as, "I sometimes was mean to her." Other things may come to the surface:

"Why was I unable to recognize his symptoms?"

"She is so frail lying there, and I can't help her."

"If I had done other things, would our marriage have held together?"

"Is my child gay because of me?"

"Have I been kind enough in explaining my lifestyle to my family?"

Of course, being gay is not a disease or something shameful. There are, however, people who need to understand what it is to be gay. A dialogue in the group setting may help you clarify your feelings. You will go away with input from others that will hopefully strengthen your ability to communicate with your loved ones.

Remember, although the need to blame yourself is not unusual, most of the time it is undeserved. Most people tend to fall into this trap when looking for an answer to the inevitable "Why?" that lurks in the minds of all who are grieving.

By this time, you will have grown to know your fellow support group members well. After all, you have been sharing intimate thoughts about your pain and anger. When you choose to verbalize your guilt feelings, recognize just how helpful your group can be. The participants are not there to sit in judgment on your attitudes. They are there to do just what they—and you—set out to do: receive and offer support.

Sometimes people will blurt out things that are meaningless but that can hurt dreadfully because they can stifle your sense of freedom to express yourself.

They say things like, "Don't feel that way."

People have the right to feel any way they choose,

and this includes you! Your facilitator should intervene if inappropriate comments are being made.

You can expect others to acknowledge your painful sharing and indicate some understanding of how difficult it has been. It is unlikely that anyone in the group will fail to understand what you are saying. In one form or another, they are experiencing similar emotions.

There are any number of situations that can bring on feelings of guilt. For example, you may have placed your special person in a nursing home and now feel uncomfortable about this decision. If that person has died, you may well have forgotten what made you decide to place her there in the first place. It is important to remember.

Perhaps finances did not permit hiring home nursing people. Perhaps your job did not afford you the hours to be available. Perhaps you could not emotionally handle the task of caring for your special person.

Bereaved parents may feel extreme guilt because embedded within the lore of parenting is the unwritten thought "I should have been able to save him or her." Parents experience guilt because they feel they have failed when they outlive their child.

These are real situations that cause pain. It is important to understand that you did the best you could. Not coming to grips with these issues could undermine your healing process.

As you discuss your feelings with the group, you will

begin to notice a subtle difference in the atmosphere. During the first few sessions, you may have detected some discomfort when you stated your situation. By now, fellow group members are probably more comfortable with the difficulties in your life.

And in their comfort lies comfort for you!

Feel free to share your thoughts and feelings with the group. You should find some measure of comfort in being heard and understood. The group and your facilitator will help you clarify your feelings:

- What guilt feelings do you carry?
- What good feelings do you recall in the relationship?
- What worked well in your relationship?
- What things were tried and dropped because they did not work for you and your special person?
- How did your relationship live up—or not live up—to your expectations?

You have been culturally conditioned to speak only well of a parent or someone who has died. You have been conditioned to keep a stiff upper lip as you endured serious illness in yourself or someone you love. Television shows and magazine articles continually remind you about your lost youth. The media and religions teach us that the world stays in step by marching two by two, and if you divorce you are marching to a different drummer.

Perhaps the great (culturally conditioned) plans you had for your child, including marriage and children in the traditional sense, have to be rethought as you come to terms with your child's homosexuality.

Unfortunately many of our simple ideas about "perfect" scenarios do not apply in most real-life situations.

No one is perfect, alive or dead.

There is nothing "wrong" with recalling times the dead person was bad-tempered, abrasive, unthinking, or unreasonable. The same holds true of a parent now unable to care for himself. If your former spouse left you, it is important to focus on an honest memory. Don't paint an unrealistically bright picture of the person who is no longer in your life. Go forward. Look ahead.

When someone whom we love undergoes drastic changes in circumstance, the only thing remaining for us is an honest memory. That memory should stand true and be cherished. Do not cloud what you remember with dishonesty, whether it makes the memory look better or worse.

Do not confuse guilt with remorse.

After verbalizing what you have always thought of as guilt, discuss whether you are really feeling guilt or remorse.

You may be surprised at your response. Guilt is self-blame and is destructive. Remorse is human and, with strong support, can be placed into perspective. Working through guilt until you are comfortable can be a heavy-duty exercise.

Your facilitator will encourage you to tell the group:

• What positive experiences did you share with your special person?
• What positive act did you perform for the person you are grieving for?

If no answer springs readily to mind, force yourself to look within. There are always good acts. It is only when you are feeling like the culprit that you refuse to acknowledge you ever did anything correctly.

Positive interactions between you and your special person need not be things of epic proportions. An old song reminds us that little things mean a lot. This is especially good to remember when you are trying to find a more comfortable inner place that is free of guilt. Think of those little things:

• Did you smile at a shared joke?
• Did you take the time to call?
• Did you invite your special person to dinner?
• Did you try to visit?
• Did you buy a special food or snack?

• Did you watch a television show your special person enjoyed?

Life is comprised of moments. They are what make up our experiences. Very few of us save people from fires or robberies. Very few of us live lives of great drama.

Most of us fill our days with ordinary things. When we are grieving, however, we often discount the ordinary things. We think, rather, that we should have done something large and special and powerful. But few of us have such opportunities or abilities. Instead we have small kindnesses that we are able to give.

When you are feeling most guilty about the "should haves" and "could haves," it is important to remember this.

You were not called on to stop your mother from jumping out a window, but when she had lost her alertness you did stop her from walking into a street crowded with traffic. One act seems more heroic than the other. But in reality your mother could have been killed in either episode. One is extremely rare; the other, while mundane, is more common.

Just because something is common does not mean it is unimportant. When you are beating up on yourself for omissions, remember how necessary the ordinary is.

Sometimes there are concrete steps we can take that will aid us in our healing work. When you get home after attending this meeting, please use the page at the end of this section to list the small kindnesses you may have performed for your special person. Large favors you may have done should, of course, be mentioned, but the little things count for a great deal. You will be surprised at how much you have done when you begin to keep lists.

Once you have completed the list, look back over it when the "guilts" get you. The list will serve as your reminder that you did indeed function well in your relationship with your special person.

If you have brought photographs this week, please share them with your fellow group members.

Sometimes in the course of group participation you come to see yourself in a different light than you thought possible. By this session, notice if your behavior varies greatly from that of others in the group. Perhaps you feel such pain about things left undone that you cannot work on this point or go forward with it.

If this is what you are experiencing, if you feel you are more intense than others by a wide margin, then you may wish to consider private counseling along with group involvement.

Your facilitator can furnish a list of helping professionals to choose from.

Guilt and its repercussions can leave strong and painful feelings that last for years. The support group cannot remove those feelings, but it can help you learn to accept your situation and understand what you can reasonably hold yourself responsible for.

The philosopher Erich Fromm explained this succinctly when he said, "The psychic task which a person can and must set for himself is not to feel secure but to be able to tolerate insecurity."

If the group has given you this ability to tolerate insecurity and loss then it has indeed fulfilled its mission.

Make this list as long as you wish. You will probably need more than one sitting to think and make a complete list. Be kind to yourself. Be fair. See if you can continue and fill the page.

My Kind Acts Toward _____

_____

_____

_____

_____

_____

_____

_____

_____

_____

_____

_____

_____

Things I Learned at This Meeting:

_____

_____

_____

_____

_____

_____

The Point I Wish to Make at the Next Meeting:

_____

_____

_____

_____

_____

_____

_____

Meeting Five

DEPRESSION

And our hearts, though stout and brave,
Still, like muffled drums, are beating
Funeral marches to the grave.

—HENRY WADSWORTH LONGFELLOW

Your facilitator will begin this meeting by asking if you would care to share some of your list of kindnesses, from last week's meeting, with other members of the group. You might be surprised to see how much your lists have in common. This knowledge can be strengthening.

If you do not wish to share your entire list, or if you wish to keep it private, the choice is yours. However, people tend to find that the more they share, the more they benefit.

As you reflect on the items on the list, you will probably experience pangs of sadness once again, and that is not unusual. You are in the group, after all, to work through your feelings. If sadness comes over you again, it is perfectly natural.

This sense of sadness is different from depression. Sadness is somewhat gentler than depression and should be understood as such. It is usually triggered by a specific event and is a temporary feeling. If, for instance, you are marking the tenth anniversary of your son's death you will feel sad. Your heart may be heavy and you may cry. The feeling will stay with you for a limited amount of time and then you will go on with your life. The feeling of sadness will have lifted.

Unless you work through it, depression does not lift. It is everywhere. It is there when the flowers are riotous in color, when a child is confirmed, when a beloved child becomes a parent. Regardless of the joyousness of the event, depression sits always at hand.

Depression has a character and power all its own.

While it does not sound as gut-wrenching as anger or guilt, depression is without question an extremely debilitating emotion. It can leave the person who experiences it bereft. It may well be the most intense and invasive emotion anyone experiences, after the devastation of loss.

You may already have become familiar with depression and its many manifestations. They include

- Tension
- Insomnia
- Feelings of worthlessness
- Bitter self-accusation

This is the short list. A longer list follows at the end of this section. It may be helpful to name your sensations so you can identify what you are feeling. It is also helpful to know with some certainty that your thoughts are not unique to you. Somewhere someone else is also thinking and writhing in similar pain.

"Why go on?"

"There is no point to anything anymore."

"It is just too hard to get moving."

"I will do as little as possible to just get by."

"What is life all about anyway?"

You may be feeling a sense of futility. It may seem that the hurt that will never go away.

Such emotions, frequently passionate in their intensity, are normal. They are real sentiments, and they are honest. As you have searched your soul for ways to help yourself, you have probably felt great depression.

If your decision-making ability seems to be affected, it may or may not matter in small things. But if you are making life changes because of your loss, how your depression impacts on your life can be of great significance.

Sometimes the depression begins to fit almost like a second skin. Even painful issues can become so familiar that you carry them into everything you do. Depression can become such a permanent part of you that it can almost feel comfortable, because it feels familiar when everything else around you feels alien and strange.

Depression can become such a part of you that you do not even notice the changes in your facial expression. You may not notice how sad your eyes look. It is almost as if they have always been that way.

Depression listens, just as you listen to what others say. At one time in your life, a time before your pain began, you might have responded in a certain manner. Now, more often than not, *you* do not respond. Your depression answers for you.

When it is deep enough, your depression can *become* you.

Depression can come with the knowledge that you will have to restructure your life without the presence of your special person. You may feel very much alone.

Depression can come with the knowledge that you will have to adapt to a new way of life, such as no longer being a part of the workforce. Now you are on your own. It can feel frightening. A period of depression can be a dreadful time to make career decisions that should be decided by a bright and clear-thinking mind.

"Where do I go from here?" is a question that circles round and round in the morass of pain and lack of clarity you are experiencing. How can anyone make decisions about the future when in such a bog?

A gay person coming out to his or her family for the first time may have questions that are better dealt with once he or she has worked through the emotional issues, questions such as "Do I come out to others?" "Do I change the way I live my life?" "Am I better off not sharing with anyone?"

Similarly, family members might wonder what changes they should make. Fortunately we have come a great distance over the past decade or two, and maybe before long these questions will not be as burning and painful. People will accept themselves more lovingly, and perhaps society will follow this lead.

Perhaps you have recently been told you are suffering a debilitating or terminal illness. While you may wish to cherish every moment you have while you can still get around and live a productive life, you now have a new reality to come to terms with. When you have been given such information, make sure those around you understand the magnitude of your situation. If the diagnosis is terminal, those who love you will lose a friend. But you will lose everyone. Who can blame you for feeling anxious and depressed?

If you have been told you have a debilitating illness that will have a rapid progression, that news also can help increase your depression. How will you cope? Will you be able to work?

Whatever your situation, all the emotions owned by others in your group are yours as well. Use the support of these people and listen to how they are trying to work out their lives. There may be many things of value that you will be able to incorporate into your personal situation and way of coping.

While you are depressed, you will find it difficult to

roll up your sleeves and work with whatever issues are on the horizon. The support group is there to help you work *through* the depression and into a time where clarity becomes your ally.

To make things more difficult, sometimes your depression can push others away and not allow you to receive support or comfort from loved ones.

You may be thinking, "Where are all my friends when I need them?" You may not realize that you have contributed to their absence. Your support people are absent not because they do not wish to help. More likely, they are absent because you have rendered them powerless to offer you anything that may seem even remotely positive.

In reality, there may well come a time when your friends are no longer able to help you even by listening. They are worn out. They have listened. They have been there. They have offered suggestions that most likely went unheeded because you were incapable of action. And, yes, gradually they did begin to draw away and call less frequently.

This is where your support group can be especially helpful. Members can fill in for your friends and other loved ones as you discuss whether you might be partially responsible for your isolation.

Since recovering from the pain of loss is not an exact science, there is no hard-and-fast rule that you will indeed experience this or any emotion discussed thus far.

Depression, however, is a common experience following a drastic change in your circumstances, whether you are dealing with the death of a loved one, an aging or ill parent, a divorce, a job loss, rejection because you are gay, or your own illness.

In the group setting, it is not helpful to make your feelings trivial. Do not downplay them. *Do not invalidate yourself!*

In daily life, if you are feeling this insidious emotion and you are asked what is wrong, you are apt to reply, "Oh, I'm *just* depressed." Within the group, it is safe to say you are depressed and it hurts terribly, or that you are depressed and feel *nothing*. The numbing type of depression is as hurtful as a depression that has you reeling with emotion.

You will discover that many things trigger depression anew. Some people are affected by a change in seasons. You may have such thoughts as these:

- It is spring and he is dead.
- She loved winter so and now doesn't recognize it.
- When we were married, summer and surfing were so special to us.
- Our whole family got together for Memorial Day and now we are no longer a united clan.
- Everyone is waking up and getting dressed for work, but I have no place to go.

Such thoughts are not uncommon. Others have had these feelings in the past. Sadly, others in the future will feel what you are feeling today. You are not alone. You now have a group with whom you may share your hurt.

Again, there is strength to be drawn from numbers.

As any person who has experienced a loss can attest, birthdays and holidays often intensify our painful experiences. Even worse, however, is the buildup to a holiday. Our anticipation of how painful it will be is nearly always worse than the reality.

Your facilitator will understand this and ask group members who have lived through at least a year of life-cycle events to share experiences and helpful suggestions for those who are facing holidays for the first time since their lives have changed. If a special event is due to take place soon after this session, you may wish to bring a picture or other memento and ask the group to take a minute to honor your anxiety.

Anytime you are willing to share something, you will aid the entire group. Perhaps you have changed your mealtime at holidays or rearranged the furniture or menu and have felt your heart lighten. Share these innovations because you may be throwing someone a lifeline.

If something comes to mind outside the meeting, please use the page at the end of this section to make a note of it.

Do not be surprised if you cry during this session. Any discussion about depression may bring on tears. Don't be afraid of your own tears or those of other members. *Tears are only liquid emotion and can be cleansing.*

If your tears prevent you from speaking at any time, either shake your head or indicate that the group leader should go to the person seated next to you. When you feel comfortable you will rejoin the conversation.

Some members of the group may be depressed and frozen in their emotion. They may not cry. They may state their case articulately. Do not judge them or think they are not in pain. Each person expresses his or her depression differently. What is important is that it does not remain bottled up but is expressed in some appropriate manner.

At the end of this section is a list of words that describe specific emotions you may be feeling while depressed. Your facilitator will ask you to turn to that page, look at the words, and circle those that seem to fit your experience best.

When you have finished going through the list, the group will talk about the words each of you feels best describe your feelings.

After the meeting, take some time to look over the list again. You may feel inspired to write a little about what certain words mean. You may even wish to begin a journal because your depression may take a different form each time you look over the list.

Identifying what you are feeling in such a visual way is an important step in getting through the depression.

As you go through the word list, please remember this statement by Ralph Waldo Emerson: "A man becomes what he thinks about all day long."

The List

Surging of emotion	*Loss of appetite*
Bitterness	*Anxiety*
Fear	*Rage*
Anguish	*Futility*
Sadness	*Attention-span problem*
Resentment	*Disappointment*
Dejection	*Helplessness*
Disbelief	*Nervousness*
Weight loss	*Yearning*
Resignation	*Numbness*
Panic	*Sleeplessness*
Physical reactions	*Despair*
Forgetfulness	*Talkativeness*
Hypochondria	*Loneliness*
Hopelessness	*Hostility*
Agitation	*Guilt*
Sorrow	*Emptiness*
Regret	*Inability to make choices*

Things I Learned at This Meeting:

_____

_____

_____

_____

_____

_____

_____

The Point I Wish to Make at the Next Meeting:

_____

_____

_____

_____

_____

_____

_____

Helpful Holiday Changes

_____

_____

_____

_____

_____

_____

_____

_____

_____

_____

_____

_____

Meeting Six

POWERLESSNESS

I could not stop something I knew was wrong and terrible. I had an awful sense of powerlessness.

—ANDREI SAKHAROV

When someone grieves deeply the change of a circumstance that involves a loss, one of the most frustrating emotions he or she will experience is that of powerlessness.

Many people go through life feeling they have some control over events. They are comfortable knowing they have a choice about any number of things. Even if they do not like their job, they did have a choice before starting it!

When a loved one dies, that control seems to have vanished, leaving in its stead a feeling of devastation.

The same is true if your aging parent becomes less functional, or if you yourself are aging.

When a marriage or relationship ends, regardless of who initiated the break, you may feel deeply unsettled.

If you are dealing with a homosexual issue, you may well have wished for different circumstances, believing that things would be easier if you or your loved one were straight. But, as you have come to understand, human beings are what they are, and none of us has the power to change anyone or anything other than how we react to life events.

Illness leaves its own deep mark on you and those

around you. If you have been given a troubling report by the doctor, it may be empowering for a while to look for second opinions and even explore how others have handled your ailment. Regardless of what you do medically, the emotional component of powerlessness remains: How do I regain control of my own body?

Powerlessness can be among the most undermining of feelings. "All the king's horses and all the king's men couldn't put Humpty Dumpty together again." In other words, despite trying with all your being to find the right doctors, to offer the best environment, or to work at being as supportive as possible, you could not help the one you love or change the circumstances of your life or theirs.

Unfortunately people who are hurting sometimes associate powerlessness with failure. Not only do they feel guilty, angry, or depressed, they also feel worthless. They see the problem as a manifestation of their own shortcomings. So, in addition to facing the brutal truth of their particular difficulty, they all too often feel they "should have been able to prevent it."

Powerlessness works hand in hand with guilt but is actually a separate experience. Acknowledging this will enable you to deal with the issues over which you do have some control.

There are many painful feelings associated with powerlessness. They include:

- Anger
- Rage
- Frustration
- Fear
- Despair
- Hysteria

Your facilitator will ask each of you if you have experienced or are experiencing these things. If other words describing feelings come to mind at this time, share them with the group.

Powerlessness has the ability to make a hurting person feel very small and insignificant. When someone feels this way, they have lost that necessary sense of being in charge of their own life. It is the way a child feels when faced with a project that is overwhelming.

Success is another factor that contributes mightily to the problem of feeling powerless. Often a man or woman who has risen through the corporate ranks, carved out his or her own business, or accomplished much in a field like medicine, education, religion, or the law has an especially hard time coping with powerlessness. After all, he or she has created a world tailored to certain specifications. Now all that success goes for nothing.

Women who have stayed at home rather than go into the business world face a similar problem. These women have given their lives to those around them, running a household and serving as nurturers. They have bandaged cut fingers, comforted men who feared the next step up the corporate ladder, or mended and tended children and the terminally ill.

Their roles were always fairly well defined, and they worked well within them. Now the person they tended is no longer around to need them, or they cannot meet the person's new needs. When they are faced with the change in someone they loved, they also see it as a change in a way of life. When they no longer have a familiar role, they feel helpless.

Situations involving another party or bad luck can imbue powerlessness with great rage. Perhaps a special person was killed by a drunk driver who received a mere slap on the wrist for this atrocity. Perhaps your mother slipped on a soapy floor and received a head injury that permanently damaged her thinking power.

In cases like these, where there may be someone to blame, grieving people need to feel that justice has been done. It is crucial for their healing that this matter be resolved in some appropriate way. Without resolution, powerlessness is heightened and the pain goes on.

The facilitator will ask you questions about your sense of powerlessness:

- Did you feel insignificant?
- How did you handle that feeling emotionally?

• Did you take any action?
• Was it helpful?

Your group will probably have many different experiences to share. If a group member is feeling small or, at the other end of the scale, is raging, ask what he or she believes would be helpful. The group may offer creative support and encourage action.

In the case of an outrageously light sentence when a legal judgment is involved, some group member may suggest writing to the prosecutor or judge.

Most professional associations have grievance committees. In medical situations, the state medical association might prove helpful. If the difficulty is with a lawyer, the state bar association might respond with action.

Ask for group support if you choose to take an action. The input may be helpful.

When you write letters or make telephone calls to express your disappointment or anger, you show yourself that you are *not* powerless. There are things *you can do* even when the situation is disastrous.

Life is not fair, but you *do* have the right to seek justice. You may not get it, but you have the right to try.

On the other hand, if you are feeling uncertain about how you handled a situation or how one should be handled, someone may suggest you get back in touch with the authority who handled your special person's case. He or she may be able to remind you once again of why your action was appropriate, which will help you in your effort to heal.

If you have made the tough decision to place someone you love in a nursing home, you may need affirmation that you did the right thing.

If you are feeling frustrated watching your body become less functional, you truly understand powerlessness. Certainly not everyone has a difficult time as they age, but your own reality must be your guide. How you handle your infirmity is your choice. You may choose to whine and complain to your family and friends. You may choose to be secretive. Or you may choose to let them see you smile.

You may find it helpful to bring your complaints to the group. It is possible that those close to you have stopped hearing you with respect because they have heard you so often. You may find that expressing yourself to those open to listening makes you feel powerful again.

When all is said and done, there is no person alive who likes to feel powerless. Even small children try to assert their power. It is an innate yearning for any human being.

Sometimes we are fortunate and, after we get through the pain, can regain our sense of control over events.

We must always remember, though, that not all events can be controlled. Some are simply out of our hands. Any time we hear about a fatal accident or read the obituaries, this fact is reinforced.

We can control only our own actions and behaviors. Let us hope that it will be enough to make us less frustrated and more comfortable.

Groucho Marx said, "Each morning when I open my eyes, I say to myself, 'I, not events, have the power to make me happy or unhappy today. I can choose which it shall be. Yesterday is dead, tomorrow hasn't arrived yet. I have just one day, today, and I'm going to be happy in it.'"

Things I Learned at This Meeting:

_____

_____

_____

_____

_____

_____

_____

The Point I Wish to Make at the Next Meeting:

_____

_____

_____

_____

_____

_____

_____

Things I Learned At This Meeting

The Point I Want to Make at the Next Meeting

Meeting Seven

ACCEPTANCE

To learn to live without certainty and yet without being paralyzed by hesitation is to learn the lesson of acceptance.

—ANONYMOUS

As a participant in a support group, whether you are a facilitator or member, you have gained insights into the dynamics of mourning and grief.

By your presence and willingness to listen, you have helped yourself and others to become vocal and active in a situation where the choice might have been silent suffering.

You have learned to understand and share your innermost attitudes about loss or about a special person for whom you cared deeply.

One of the primary goals of a support group is to help you identify the different emotions you are experiencing.

We have all heard someone say, "Let me do one thing at a time." When you examine emotional issues layer by layer, they become easier to understand. If all that you see is a large cluster of pain, it is often more difficult to separate out and deal with the emotions the hurt brings about.

We have discussed denial, which is the conditioned response to the news of a major change or difficult life event.

Some of you may have started attending sessions

while still in this state. You may have heard things that made no real impact during the first meeting but that now have penetrated.

You have talked about foolish things people say in their efforts to be helpful. This has probably come up in most sessions.

You have dealt in some depth with anger and the large role it plays in the process of grief.

Another important issue is religion. You have probably brought into focus many ambivalent feelings toward faith and God. You may have come away feeling more intensely about God, or you may be convinced there is no such supreme being.

You understand that no one is in a position to judge what someone else feels about any issue, and that especially includes the question of God.

Although it is painful, you discussed openly the issue of guilt and how profound its impact can be. When you are dealing with great pain, guilt has its own irony. As if they feel they have not suffered enough, many people who are hurting force themselves to find things about which to feel guilty.

Depression, and its potential for long-term harm, has been the focal point of one meeting and has probably been introduced by group members into others.

The sensation of powerlessness looms heavily throughout any discussion of grief. The feeling that you are small and the world is big and unpredictable may be frightening. Hopefully the group has helped you see that you do indeed matter. You have a rightful place within your own group of friends and family. Perhaps now you will be more comfortable taking that place.

You will now be working toward the hoped-for end stage in the grief process: acceptance.

Acceptance has been defined as the net result of a healthy grief process. It is the ability to recall your special person without pain, to think about your special circumstances realistically and without mourning. Acceptance does not proceed from denying the loss or change, but rather through confronting the event.

The only way around grief is through it!

No one expects pain to vanish completely after the group meetings end. That is not the way it generally works. What is hoped is that you can separate and identify the emotion you are feeling at any given time, and that you now have the resources within you to face it.

If you are new to your grief, you may have benefited from hearing from those whose lives were altered some time earlier. Those going through the meeting process a second time have probably been able to offer valuable insights into how people feel who are experiencing the pain of the process.

Newcomers attend with fresh insights. If your painful memories were not resolved when you decided to come to the group, bringing them to the fore has given you the opportunity to explore them and possibly put them to rest.

Each person in the group has served as a role model to the others. Hopefully many participants were positive models. But it is also possible to learn what you do not wish to become. You might have seen great bitterness, heard harsh and ugly sentiments, hatred, and other negative emotions expressed by people in pain.

Hearing them and seeing them gives you the opportunity to make a choice about your own conduct. Do you wish to be that type of person?

Can your loving nature come through your difficult ordeal intact? Will you always be stuck in bitterness?

Remember, acceptance does not mean liking the situation. It merely means one has come to understand it and to be less frightened by it.

While some have called acceptance the result of a healthy grief process, your facilitator will ask how you define it personally. What does acceptance mean to you?

- Have you reached the stage of acceptance?
- Were there any special things you did that were not discussed at the meeting?
- Did people outside the group help?
- What kind of support really *helped*?

• Have you taken the time to thank the people in your life who stood by you when you needed them?

If you have not done so, now would be a good time to compile a list of people to thank and then to do so by telephone or letter. A page for your list has been provided at the end of this section.

Your facilitator will urge you to continue to set aside time to deal with your pain. If you use this time wisely and *daily,* it can help you work toward acceptance, because you will be working *through* your grief and not around it.

Going through the process of acceptance is not for the meek. It takes great courage to go forward. You are acknowledging that you are still a factor in the universe.

Going forward and backward is all part of the healing process. It is time to take action in your life, to do things, even small things, that have meaning. You have not failed if something does not work for you; if you find it difficult to get out of the place that is full of hurt. What is important is that you pick up the pieces and walk forward again.

Some people prefer to remain in the place of their pain. They feel safe with what they know. It is much easier for them, even if what they know is pain, to remain where they are than to move forward into an unfamiliar world.

The group might share ideas of action, such as the following:

- Go to a restaurant, even if it is only for coffee.
- Go to a movie.
- Make plans in advance, although not too far in advance. The expected pain of "tomorrow" will be softened if you know there will be something that needs doing.

One of the greatest deterrents to healing and acceptance is the fear that if you try to move on with your life you will be leaving your special person behind all alone.

Your facilitator will ask if you have this fear. The group may help you find some coping skills to aid you in going forward.

Have you had this sensation? If so, share it with the group. If others have not yet identified this feeling, it does need to be discussed.

Have you gone back to work? Gone grocery shopping? Paid your bills? The time is approaching when longer-range chores should be addressed. Perhaps it is time to:

- Balance your checkbook.
- Buy that overdue gift.
- Clean your closet.

- Repair that leaking faucet.
- Get a haircut.
- Read the newspaper.
- Deep clean a room.

After a while you will be comfortable with these steps. It is then time to challenge yourself once again.

- Rearrange your furniture.
- Sort through the clothing you have stockpiled, and give away those things you do not need. It is okay to keep some item because it reminds your of your bond with your special person.
- Look for new hobbies, especially ones that are creative, like woodworking, knitting, sculpting, drawing, perhaps even painting by numbers.

Have you tried any of these projects? What was the result? Did they help? Are you further along in your healing?

Sometimes you may make efforts or try things that do not work out. This is not shameful, nor is it unusual. If you have some thoughts about why your effort failed, please share them. Someone in the group may benefit from your experience.

If you are a widow or your husband has Alzheimer's, was your first time out alone painful? Did you have to leave a restaurant because you were in tears? If so, please try again when you are ready.

Perhaps your next effort can be smaller. Other members may offer suggestions. Any step you take will enhance the quality of your life. Do not stop taking steps, even if you have to make them smaller and safer ones.

Another stage of acceptance is regrouping and strengthening the family unit.

- Have you paid much attention to how those around you are dealing with your painful circumstance?
- Have any of these people taken a step that had a productive outcome?

It's impossible to ignore holidays and anniversaries. They will not be easy. Just be certain that your anticipation will be worse than the reality. This is nearly always the case. You will probably need to go through an entire year of such events to see the proof of this.

Your facilitator will encourage those who have made holiday changes that were helpful to share them.

There may be other actions to take to help others and help yourself heal:

- On the page provided at the end of this section, list three small tasks you will undertake each week for four weeks.
- If you are financially able to do so, you may walk

the path to acceptance by establishing foundations or giving grants.
- Visit orphanages.
- Help in a school classroom.
- Donate unneeded wheelchairs or other appliances.
- Volunteer at a nursing home.
- If you feel ready to take in information, enroll in an adult education class.

This meeting is meant to allow for closure. You have taken loose ends and woven them together. You are taking action and moving forward. If you wish to go through the support group process again, it may be helpful for you to work with another facilitator. You may gain yet another perspective.

We can be like the Dead Sea, which receives fresh water daily, yet retains it and gives nothing back in return. Or we can be like the Sea of Galilee, which nurtures the fruit trees and the lands it touches. By giving to others, by enriching the life around us, *we* become richer, better, and more loved.

Take hands and congratulate yourselves. You have completed the program.

Things I Learned at This Meeting:

_____

_____

_____

_____

_____

_____

_____

People I Want to Call or Write
and Thank for Their Support

_____

_____

_____

_____

_____

_____

Three Small Tasks I Will Undertake
Each Week for Four Weeks

WEEK ONE

1. _____

2. _____

3. _____

WEEK TWO

1. _____

2. _____

3. _____

WEEK THREE

1. _____

2. _____

3. _____

WEEK FOUR

1. _____

2. _____

3. _____

Organizing a Support Group

Organizing a Support Group

How to Find a Support Group

If you have made the decision to join a support group but don't know how to find one, you may be surprised as the number of resources there are.

Many professionals in nearly every field "support" support groups. They find them a positive adjunct to their own work. Clergy people are frequently asked for support by members of their congregations. They are asked when a family member dies, when there are difficulties with aging parents, when marriages are troubled, when a family member is gay.

Since congregations are frequently large and there are limited numbers of clergy, it is not possible for one person to provide ongoing support to each individual member. Therefore, many churches and synagogues sponsor support groups.

People dealing with a serious illness or the death of a loved one may ask doctors where they can go to find comfort. A doctor can also serve as a good referral source if one sees a parent or spouse in turmoil over a life-changing event. Many hospitals now see the benefits of support groups and offer them or make space available for such meetings. A hospital social worker can help you get involved.

More and more nursing homes hold meetings that benefit both residents and family members and serve as a natural part of the care of the resident. Guardians who work with the aging population as well as senior citizen housing administrators and retiree organizations can usually refer family members to groups.

Funeral directors sometimes sponsor groups. This excellent public service helps many grieving people. Such meetings are usually held in private homes, though some are held in churches.

Civic organizations, including Lions Clubs and women's auxiliaries, help support groups in their communities. Most organizations have a physical facility where meetings are held.

As employees who are under great pressure are generally less effective in their jobs, corporations sponsor support groups, often through employee assistance programs.

Lawyers who work with families dealing with loss through accident or illness are often able to refer clients to a group.

If you are in need of a support group, you can usually find one by contacting any of the above organizations, or by asking caring friends. Word of mouth may be your best resource.

How to Gather Participants

If you are a person who initiates and if you feel ready to take action, you may want to create your own group.

All of the people and organizations mentioned in the previous section are good resources for names of potential participants. Many professionals look for a helping place to which they might send those in need. If you are interested in forming a group, you may seek out people in the professions noted above and leave your information with them. Generally they will ask permission before giving you a name, or they may have people contact you directly.

Newspapers run health-tip columns that might mention your group.

Many organizations that deal with specific illnesses, such as cancer foundations, lung associations, or Alzheimer's disease groups, have names of people who could benefit from support. Let them have your information. Often their mailing lists are extensive.

Try to promote your group by speaking at civic functions, or appearing on local talk shows, or cable television interview shows.

Place information in the newsletters of churches, social organizations, clubs and similar broad-based organizations, or in community bulletins or union publications.

How to Structure the Meetings

Meetings should be held every week at the same time, if possible in the same place.

It is helpful to greet people at the door for the first few meetings. Most people are timid about taking this step. A firm handshake and perhaps an introduction to someone else can be welcoming and put people at ease.

When possible, ask that family members attend separate meetings. If a husband and wife come to the meeting together because their child has died, it is helpful if they are either in separate groups or at least *do not sit next to one another.* Frequently one or the other will become the spokesperson for both. When this occurs, the person who is silent is not representing him- or herself but is being represented by the spouse.

The same is true if a mother and daughter come together. The mother may not feel the freedom that she needs to discuss her relationship with her late husband in front of her daughter. Perhaps there was infidelity that the daughter doesn't need to know about.

Ideally your group should not exceed twelve people. You might even prefer six or seven. People benefit when they feel they have been heard. When there are too many participants in the group, answers must be abbreviated in order to allow everyone a fair opportunity to share experiences, especially within a limited period of time.

Limit each session to *two hours*.

Start promptly and end promptly. It's critical to offer such structure to people who feel afloat in a sea of pain.

Use name tags until you are certain everyone knows each other's first name. Last names are unnecessary. The facilitator should also wear a name tag. Calling people by their correct name is not only courteous, it is welcoming.

Arrange chairs in a circle so everyone is visible to everyone else.

You may also place in the center of the circle a table containing a box of tissues, a pitcher of water, and some cups.

Group members will find it useful to have their own manuals, as there are places in the book where they can make notes.

Each person might also be asked to read aloud a portion of the manual. This is a good way to get people actively involved. When people read, they seem to feel more a part of the process, but no one should be pressured to read who feels uncomfortable doing so. If a member declines, the member sitting next to him or her can pick up at that point.

Your group will be at its best when it is well-structured and run by a caring and attentive facilitator.

How to Become a Facilitator

If you are looking for a facilitator for your group,
wish to become one, there are a number of resource
you can go to. The religious community has such information in its files. A priest or clergy person will un-
doubtedly know people of high caliber who can handle
such a task. If you are in a religious setting, avoid asking
for volunteers. People may come forward who are not
necessarily well suited to the task. Instead, *invite* quali-
fied people into your program.

An effective facilitator must read this manual care-
fully in order to understand what will be discussed. She
or he must be comfortable with the material.

One excellent way to accomplish this is for a group
of facilitators to go through the process of these sessions before leading a group, with each potential facilitator taking a turn leading a training meeting. No one
should function as a facilitator without having gone
through the program. This training will become intense. Would-be facilitators discuss their own personal
pain as part of their training. By the time they have
completed the program, they should be comfortable
with the material. If they are not, they need to go
through the program again or consider whether this
commitment is right for them.

The first item of business after you introduce yourself
to the group will be to tell them there is a code of

ing confidentiality that cannot be broken. Ask
rticipants not to share the names of fellow group
mbers outside the group. Since most people live or
ork in a community where they are known, it is important not to divulge what people say. Participants will
be hearing harsh things. Some of them will be about
family members. The function of the group is to allow
members to vent their emotions safely, without fear
that their statements will be shared and possibly do
long-range harm.

The second item of business is to explain to group
members that the major function of the sessions is to
offer a haven where people can talk about guilt and
anger and powerlessness without feeling they are being
judged. It is okay for a member who has made a statement to be challenged about what he or she has expressed as long as the challenge is not judgmental. If
people begin to feel judged, they will not feel safe, and
they will ultimately lose faith in the group and the
facilitator.

Group leaders are not therapists. They are there to lend
structure to the meetings and to help people verbalize
their feelings. It is absolutely out of the province of the
facilitator to advise on anything other than seeking individual counseling. This is always true unless the group
is run by a licensed therapist who feels comfortable taking on the role of advisor.

If a member asks a direct question about how to

handle a situation, the best advice the facilitator offer is what would apply from his or her personal perience. When you as the facilitator offer that expe rience, be sure to remind members that you are not telling them that your experience is the "right" way of handling a situation. You are simply sharing one way of responding.

Since everyone has a loss or significant life change at one time or another, it is possible to function well as a facilitator despite not having experienced the particular issue a member may be dealing with.

Be warned, though. If you have *not* experienced the same issue (if you are not a bereaved parent, for example), never tell those who are in the situation that you know how they feel. You do not. You are there because you are a kind and giving person who wishes to help people deal with a process that in some cases is impossible for them to deal with alone. "I know how you feel" is a *major red flag* and could alienate the group from you at the outset.

By all means share your own experiences freely when they apply. You may also call on the experiences of people you know, if it seems appropriate.

Before your first meeting, gather a list of good mental health people who specialize in the different problem areas this manual addresses. If possible, cross–check each individual with more than one other mental health person. Rabbi Dannel Schwartz of Temple Shir Shalom

st Bloomfield, Michigan, suggests that the best
to find an expert is to ask other experts and cross-
eck the names you are given.

Keep this list up to date, and always have it with you at the meeting. You might be asked by a participant for the name of someone who offers private counseling.

On the other hand, you might see that someone is in deeper distress than a group is able to handle. Some people may be experiencing such great trauma that a structured gathering place in which to talk out issues and problems will simply not be enough. In such a case, speak to the person in private and tactfully suggest that he or she seek individual counseling. You can tell this person that the group will be available when the counselor feels he or she is ready to participate.

It might be helpful to make notes after the first meeting. It will help you remember what distress each person is experiencing. If necessary, make the notes during the meeting. It's critical to remember each person's pain throughout the meeting and all the meetings to follow.

If a group member begins to cry, please do not offer tissues. The person can reach for them when he or she is ready. Some therapists believe that when a tissue is offered the person is being given a silent signal to stop crying.

Language is very important, and so are terms. They

can help us clarify feelings. Thomas P. Lynch, an expert on grief, has some excellent definitions, which are expanded upon below in the context of support groups. This is especially useful for facilitators.

Bereavement This is a period of time following the death of an important person. It says nothing of the quality or duration of emotion, but only signifies a date within a personal history.

Bereavement is also the "event" in the personal history that triggers the emotion of grief. There are forms of bereavement other than death that need to be honored. A serious illness and the loss of some bodily function are also bereavement issues. Divorce, too, is such an event.

There are also those who feel bereft at the loss of their youth.

When a gay person comes out, straight friends and family often feel bereft. They may have had dreams of grandchildren and nieces and nephews that probably will now not come about. On the other hand, when the information is not received lovingly or delivered lovingly, the homosexual person may also be bereft. In many cases, those who were staunch friends cannot cope with the information and the structure is broken. The same may apply to family members.

Mourning This is the process of recovery and adjustment to loss. Mourning is the method by which the powerful emotions engendered by loss are slowly and painfully brought under control.

Such emotions can also come into play with aging, long-term ailments, and watching the progression of a debilitating disease in someone you care about. They can be there as you watch your marriage disintegrate or when you have been rocked by shattering news. While you mourn, you are still in the process of adjusting.

Mourning is not limited to the loss of a parent, child, or spouse. It can be for a friend, a job, or a way of life.

Grief This is the response to any loss or separation, real or imagined, actual or symbolic, of any emotionally significant person, object, or situation that is perceived to be of an irretrievable or permanent nature. Grief is always more than sorrow. It is the raw feeling at the center of a process that engages a person who is adjusting to changed circumstances. This feeling takes on several aspects, including the deep fears of the obstacles one faces after a significant loss and the need to find a new way of life.

Take one definition at a time, and during the first group meeting ask members how they feel about the definitions. You may help draw them out by asking for their input on these terms, and it may be helpful to review them in later sessions.

If your group is sponsored by a religious organization, you may wish to close each session with a shor healing prayer. Your minister, priest, or rabbi can help select something appropriate or you may have poems and sayings that are personal favorites. Feel free to close the meeting with one that you deem fitting. Invite group members to bring in and share other inspirational thoughts.

At the end of each meeting, announce the topic of the next session, so that members can think about the issue beforehand.

As the weeks progress, you will notice that certain people have gravitated to one another. You may be asked whether outside friendships are a good idea. In most instances they are very helpful. People may go for coffee after the meeting. This is very common in groups like Alcoholics Anonymous. Some members of AA have said that intense discussion goes on during such post-meeting get-togethers.

But in the early sessions, people should be a bit cautious. Being in a group is a new experience to most, and other people's anger and rage might best be handled in the group setting rather than over coffee, where there is no one to help balance the discussion. Later, of course, such outings may become natural. The bonding is strong and lifelong friendships often develop.

Your reason for wanting to facilitate a group most likely comes from your own life experiences. Draw on these experiences and make them available to the

.oup. The more open you are, the better role model you become, and the more the group will open up to you and to each other.

Becoming a facilitator is rewarding and a special way of offering something to the community. You will find your own comfort level once you have gone through the program. If you find it is not for you, you have still gained because you have had a chance to express your own pain.

Finally, if you become a facilitator, you have made a commitment. You must be there for each meeting. If you see a potential conflict in your schedule, do not sign up to lead a group. *Continuity is essential.*

Go into this project with an open mind and an open heart. While it is easy to say, "Don't think like that," you will lose your people if you do so. They will not trust you because they are not there to be evaluated or judged. They are there for comfort and support.

If you have chosen to enter the support group process, you are coming from a place of goodness within yourself. Do not mask that goodness from the group by thinking it is not professional. There is nothing wrong with reflecting back pain when you are hearing about a tragedy.

It makes you human.

FOR THE BEST IN PAPERBACKS, LOOK FOR THE

In every corner of the world, on every subject under the sun, Penguin represents quality and variety—the very best in publishing today.

For complete information about books available from Penguin—including Puffins, Penguin Classics, and Arkana—and how to order them, write to us at the appropriate address below. Please note that for copyright reasons the selection of books varies from country to country.

In the United Kingdom: Please write to *Dept. JC, Penguin Books Ltd, FREEPOST, West Drayton, Middlesex UB7 0BR.*

If you have any difficulty in obtaining a title, please send your order with the correct money, plus ten percent for postage and packaging, to *P.O. Box No. 11, West Drayton, Middlesex UB7 0BR*

In the United States: Please write to *Consumer Sales, Penguin USA, P.O. Box 999, Dept. 17109, Bergenfield, New Jersey 07621-0120.* VISA and MasterCard holders call 1-800-253-6476 to order all Penguin titles

In Canada: Please write to *Penguin Books Canada Ltd, 10 Alcorn Avenue, Suite 300, Toronto, Ontario M4V 3B2*

In Australia: Please write to *Penguin Books Australia Ltd, P.O. Box 257, Ringwood, Victoria 3134*

In New Zealand: Please write to *Penguin Books (NZ) Ltd, Private Bag 102902, North Shore Mail Centre, Auckland 10*

In India: Please write to *Penguin Books India Pvt Ltd, 706 Eros Apartments, 56 Nehru Place, New Delhi 110 019*

In the Netherlands: Please write to *Penguin Books Netherlands bv, Postbus 3507, NL-1001 AH Amsterdam*

In Germany: Please write to *Penguin Books Deutschland GmbH, Metzlerstrasse 26, 60594 Frankfurt am Main*

In Spain: Please write to *Penguin Books S.A., Bravo Murillo 19, 1° B, 28015 Madrid*

In Italy: Please write to *Penguin Italia s.r.l., Via Felice Casati 20, I-20124 Milano*

In France: Please write to *Penguin France S.A., 17 rue Lejeune, F-31000 Toulouse*

In Japan: Please write to *Penguin Books Japan, Ishikiribashi Building, 2-5-4, Suido, Bunkyo-ku, Tokyo 112*

In Greece: Please write to *Penguin Hellas Ltd, Dimocritou 3, GR-106 71 Athens*

In South Africa: Please write to *Longman Penguin Southern Africa (Pty) Ltd, Private Bag X08, Bertsham 2013*